BOOKS BY THE AUTHOR

Forever Free

This title is available as a free eBook at
WiseWordWind.com

Falling Into All

Prayer Sayer Song

Rise Eyes Wise

Rise Eyes Wise

BEN R. TEETER

WISE
WORD
WIND
PRESS

Wise Word Wind Press
P.O Box 371732
San Diego, CA 92137
WiseWordWind.com

This is not a work of fiction. Names, characters, places, locations and incidents are all real and are meant to bear a relationship to real-life individuals, living and dead, and actual places, business establishments, locations, events and incidents. Any resemblance to the reader and to those he or she may know is entirely intentional.

Cover Art is a painting by Peter Everly, Untitled, Copyright 1988, used by permission.

Cover Design by Randy Gibbs

Book Layout by Golden Ratio Book Design

First Edition

Printed in the United States of America

ISBN: 979-8-9856990-0-5 (Trade Paperback)
ISBN: 979-8-9856990-1-2 (Hardcover)
ISBN: 979-8-9856990-2-9 (Ebook)

Library of Congress Control Number: 2022910109

EPIGRAPH

Now

Let
Us

Wrap
An
Essence

Up,

In
A
Word.

Let
Some
Thing
Silent

Now
Be
Heard,

Circling
The
Still,

The
Stirred.

Rise Eyes Wise

I,

The
Great
Silent

Seeing,

Wrinkle
Here

Into
Being.

Here
Is

The
Universe

That
I
Wear.

A
Man

Sits
There.

The
Slats
Of
This
House

Peer
In,

Space
Apart,

Occupy.

Stand
Open,

And

I,

Vast
Sky

3

No
Need

Ever
More

To
Fly,

When

One
Is

Already

Sky.

All
Possible
Movement

And

Absolute
Still

Are
One.

Let
No
Man

Put
Them
Asunder.

But,

Only
Pause.

In
Awe

And
Wonder.

Into

The
Quiet
Center

I
Enter.

The
Man
I
Was,

Now
Is

Melting
Away,

Un-
Missed.

All
That
Was,

Now
Is

The
Blissed.

Let
This

Atom
Spin.

I
Am

The

Still
Point

Within.

The
Infiniteness

Here

Fills,

Leaves
No
Room,

For

Mere
Plenty.

O
This,

The
Complete

Infinity,

Only
Seems

To
Man
Mind

Not
To
Be.

The
Tree

Is

Blown
Bare.

And
Then

The
Tree
Goes.

And
Then,

The
Air.

Pursuit
Of
Prosperity

Dies
Away,

Like
A

Porch
Light

Left
On,

Useless
To
Seeing,

As
Rising
Dawn,

Infinite,

Floods

All
Of
Being.

The
Countless

Continuum

Of

The
All

Contains
No
Break,

Except
That,

That

Man
Imagination

Make.

Eternal
Things,

Seemingly
Unique.

Point
Line
Ring
Sphere,

Dance
Here,

Fabricate,

In
Angel-
Speak,

This
Moment

I
Would

Listen
Here,

My
Mind
Entire

An
Ear,

The

Perfect
Word

Now

To
Hear.

Mind

Can
Dwell

In
Any

Shell.

Be
It

Heaven,
Earth,

Hell.

O
Nimble
Monkey
Mind,

How
You
Roam,

Every-
Where
At
Home.

You
Climb

High,
Far,

Wide,

Or
Go

Reaching
Nimble
Fingers

Deep
Inside

The
Very
Very
Small.

Or,

You
May

Drop
Any
Wall

And
Embrace

The
Entire
All,

And

Here

Reside.

Miniscule,

This
Man,

Here,

Upon
This
Tiny
Sphere,

Yet,

As
He
Truly
Has

No
Size,

A

Galaxy
Of
Galaxies

Resides

Within
The
Twinkle

Of
His
Eyes.

Windows,

Wiped
Clear.

Gone,

Old
Smear.

Then,

Glass
And
All

Disappear,

And

There
Is
No

'In'

Here.

The

Here
And
Now

Contains
The
I,

And
Not

The

There
And
Then.

And
So,
O
Man,

To
Know
Thy
Self,

Do
Not
Ask,

Where
And
When.

'First,

Take

Thy
Seat,'

The
Ancient
Yogi
Said.

In
This,

Done,

And
Known
Well,

Is

All

Complete.

The
Two
Hands

Of

The
Mind

Cease
Holding

And

Disappear.

Gone.

And
In
This,

Is

The
Answer

Clear.

Paradise

O
Man,

Lies,

Within

Thy

Pair
Of
Eyes.

The

All
That
Is

Is

What
Is
Being

What
Is
Here.

I
Poise

Within

This
Origin,

This
Orifice

Of
All
Artifice,

To
See
Now

The
All

Begin.

Look!

Even
The
Continents

Dance
And
Change.

A
Moment
Ago,

They
Were
Looking
Strange.

And
Before,

They
Were

A
Whirl

Of

Dust
And
Fire,

A
Wraith

Of

Energy
In
Space,

A
Wisp

Of

God
Desire,

Solidifying

As
A
Place.

Not
Merely

Here.

'Near,'

O
Man,

The
Infinite
Complete

Is
All

That
Is
Ever

That

Already
Am
I

That
I
Seek.

There
Is

No

Distant
Peak.

Let
The
Man

Go

Where

No
Man

Is.

Let
Me

Be-
Trap.

Surrender

The
Trappings

Unto

The
Perfect
One,

That
They

Not

No
Man
Lives

Upon
This
Hill,

For,
Here,

As
He
Arrives

He
Will

Disappear,

As

All

Grows
Still.

Is
It
Monday?

Or
Is
It

The
End
Of
All
Time?

For
A
Moment
There,

I
Forgot.

Yeah.

I
Get
That

A
Lot.

Bigness
Has
Eloped

With
Smallness.

Together
They
Have

Evaporated

Into

All-
Ness.

Whom

Shall
I
Name

As
Author

Of
This
Word?

Of
This
World?

What
Syllable,

What
Pronoun,

What
Consonant
Or
Vowel
Sound?

As
Now,
The
"I"
Falls

Into
The
Profound.

Fear's
Curtains

Shroud,

Crowd,

Around
A
Place

They
Define

In

The
Space,

Limitless.

No
Explanation.   Only

No
Cause.   Now

                    As
No
Also.   Is.

No
Next.

No
Not
Yet.

No
Better.

Hello,
Authority?

I
Want
To
Report
A
Theft.

Some
One

Invaded
My
Person

And

Changed
Everything.

My

Small
And
Painful

Old
Life

Is
Missing!

A
Strange

Peace   I
And
Prosperity,   Am

Even   Not
Bliss!   Here

Are   To
In   Enjoy
Its   It!
Place.

Using
My
Face.

And,
Darn!

Thank
You,

O
Perfect
True
All,

For
Erasing

What
Never
Really
Was,

And
Which

Struggled

So
Hard

To
Be.

Every
Non-
Distinction

That
You
Find,

O
Man,

Is
Another

Knot

In
Self

That

You

Un-
Bind.

The
Partisan

Draws
Line,
Just
So,

With
Toe,
In
Sand,

And
Stands
Behind,

To
Face
The
Foe.

So
It
Is,

Until

The
Sands

Are
Washed
Away,

Or
Drift,

Or
Blow.

The
Real   To
                        Conceal.
Is

Every-
Where.

And

Requires
Much
Effort

Of

Ignoring

Submerge
In
Now.

But

Cannot
Save.

Leave
Flickering
Wave

Passing
Away,

Which

You
May
Grasp,

Upon
This

Sensory
Instrument
Frame,

Is
Hung

A
Customary
Name.

Though,

But
Little

It
Can
Sense.

It
Feels
Its
Worth

To
Be
Immense,

And
Worthy
Of

A
Quick
Defense,

Should
Any
It

Defame.

O
Mind,

Why
Do
You

Contract

Into

Tight
Little
Boxes?

With

Your
Freedom

But
One
Breath
Away,

Why

Do
You
Crouch

In
A
Corner

This
Way?

O

Let
Me

Support
You

In
Being

The

Un-

Supported.

O

Linger
And
Cling

Not,

O
Celestial
Man,

To
Your

Dreaming
Of

The
Seeming
Small

Earthen
Things,

While

All
Infinity

With
You

Sings.

Time
Collapses.

The

Its
Front
And
Back,

Separation
Shadows
Vanish.

Now
Seen

The
One-
Ness
Eye

Rises
Now,

Joined,

Full
Moon,

As
This
Instant.

Pristine.

From
Within

Soul
Sphere
Skin,

This
Finest
Fine

Pin

Pops

The
Great
Bubble.

And
Now
Ends

A
World
Of
Trouble.

Up,

Sky
Clear

Past
The

Of
Singular
Seeing,

Whited

Mountain
Top,

Let
Us
Here

Of

All
Thought,

Rest,

Just
Beyond

Rising
Into
The

Being.

Touching

Finish
Line,

Runner

Disappears.

The
Day's
Weather

Clears.

The
Wave,

Having

Rushed
A-
Roar

Upon
The
Shore,

Now

Slides
Away,

Back
In
To
Sea,

While,

On
The
Strand,

The
Gravel
And
The
Sand

Go
Tumbling
Behind,

Following,

In
Noisy
Grind,

As
Willing
Slave,

As
If

Them-
Selves,

Too

To
Save,

To
Be
Free,

By

Being
Also

Sea.

You
Say,

'He
Is
Homeless.'

Not
So.
Look.

Here
Is
His
Home.

It
May
Lack

Some
Of
Your

Customary
Features.

This
Is
Just

What
His
Rent
Buys.

He
Tries.

O
Man,

All
Perfect
Knowledge

Is
Here,

Waiting
Only
For

Your
Mind,

To
Clear.

Waking
Up,

They
Say,

Can
Occur,
In
One
Day,

As
If

A
Lightening
Flash!

A
Death,
Rebirth.

A
Shattering,

A
Dash,

Of

All
The
Earth.

Or,

It
May
Dawn

Arriving
Like
Oncoming
Spring,

Slowly
Warming

Every
Thing,

With
Nights
Of
Late
Snows,

Until

One
Knows,

Full,

The
Summer
Day,

And

Hears
It
Sing.

And

Has
Become,

In
Peace,

Only

Every
Thing.

Matter,
Energy,

Even
Mind,

Our
Scientist
Sees
As

Moving
Blind.

Whence
Originates
This
Flaw?

The
Projecting
One

Will
Someday
See,

It
Was

Himself

That
Thus

He
Saw.

The
Limitless

Is
Here,

The
Typical

Being

The
Local.

With-
In

The
Mortal
Man's

Body
Of
Causes,

The
Ego
Battle

Never
Pauses,

Lamely,
Treating

The
True

As

Visiting
Guest,

At
Best.

The
Sacred
Sage,

With
A
Laugh,

Swinging
Staff,

Strikes
Stone,

A
Ringing
Tone.

A
Rush.
A
Gush,

And

Singing
Life
Pours

For
Dusty
Clan,

Who
Tire,

Wandering
Ever
Forward

For
The

Promised
Land.

One
Sound
Is
Heard

As
Many
Voices.

One
Will
Is
Felt

As
Many
Choices.

As

One
'I'
Is,

One

Rejoices.

Can
You

Point

Or
Place
Finger,

Linger
Any
Where,

On
Any
Particle

In
Any
Article,

Where

Cannot
Be
Found,

Infinitude

Profound?

Miraculous.

My

The
Infinite
World

I.

Disappears
Or
Re-
Assembles

With
The
Winking

Twinkling

Of

Perfect
Stillness

Smiles,

And

A
Universe

Dimples

All
Of
Space.

Thinking

Is
Based
On

Dividing
And
Ignoring.

Seen,

When
It
Abates,

The
All
Real

Awaits.

Thank
You,

O
Rustling
Of
Leaves

Upon
The
Trees,

Revealing
To
Me

The
Presence

Of
Air,
There.

And
Then,
Of

The
Infinity,

And,
Of
The
One.

Divinity.

Putting

Man
And
World,

These
Hungry
Jaws,

On
Pause,

Heart
At
Rest,

Midst
Perfection's
Laws,

What
Is,

Now
Is

But

The
Blessed.

Mirage
Hallucination,

Now
Seen
Through,

Cannot
Stay,

Nor
Bring

Anew,

Another

Misconstrue.

O
Wise
Ones,

Resting

On
The
Wall,

Between

The
Nothing

And

The
All,

May
I
Please

Come,

Upon
Thee,

To
Call?

A
Miracle,

Once

So
Rare,

Is
Now

All
That
I
See,

Every-
Where.

The
Kaleidoscope,
Cosmic,

Jostles,
Turns,

Again.

Eternity's
Parts

Bump,
Tumble,

Re-
Arrange,

The
Never-
Changing

Creating
Now

The

New
And
Strange.

Take
Down
The
Tent.

Fold
It
Up.

Its
Time

Came
And
Went.

Now,

Full
Of
Empty

Is

The
Cup.

Desire
Cools

When

Dropped

Into

A
Bucket

Of
Jewels.

The
World

Stills,

With
Silence,
Fills,

Its
Chimeric
Charade,

Parade
Of
Thrills,

Chills.

The
Judgement
Numbs.

A
Sleep,
Deep,

Yet
Awake,

Now

Comes.

Mind
Now

Rests
In
The
Shade

Of

All
Objects.

The
Body

Empty
Stands.

Its
Noises
Still.

Infinity
Blows

Silent
Through

Its

Bars
And
Lines,

And
Through

All
The
Laws,

That

Its
Form
Defines.

The
First
Arch-
Angel

Melts,

Back
Into

The
One
Perfect
True.

Ocean's
Motion's
Whispers

Cease.

The
Deep,

Among,

And
Un-
Touched
By,

The
Stars,

Rests
In

The
Still.

Here
Is

The
Sleep
Awake

Of

Peace.

Allow
Me
Please

To
Hold
That
Door,

For,

Your
Arms
Are
Full.

Here,

Let
Me
Just

Give
It

A
Pull.

A
'Meaning,'

Leaning
Some-
What

To
The
True,

Is

Often
Times,

The
Best

That

The
Man
Mind

Can
Do.

There
Is

An
Apex

To

This
Day,

A
Trail,
Upon
A
Whited
Peak,

Steep,

Where

Pure
Snow

Doth
Fall

In
Prism-
Perfect

Flake,

A

Bit
Of
Sense

To
Make,

To
Know,

Falling
Out
Of

The
Empty

All.

Let
Bard
Sound,

Once
Again,

The
Bawdy
Round,

Feet
Solid

On
The
Ground.

Another
Day,

His
Lighter
Lay

May
Be
Found

To
Go
Profound,

And

The
Brawling
Hall

Unto
Respect

Confound.

Here
Is
'Me'

This
Random   In
Man   The

I   Infinity.
Seem
To
Be,

A
Drifting
Cloud

Of

I
May
Hear

The
Discourse

Of
The
Sage,

In
Looking
On

A
Printed
Page,

And

Fly
Free

Of

Situation,

Time
And
Place,

And
Even
Cosmic
Age.

The
Man
Awakens

Now

To
The
Morn.

Illusion's

Grip

Gone
Is
Dark
Dream.

Is
Torn.

The
Real

Is
Born.

O

Let
The

Infinity

Ever-
Changingly

Caress.

But
Not
Thee

Possess.

Joy
Intervenes.

Worry
Wanes.

Perfect
Intelligence

Explains.

Only
Peace

Ever
Remains.

Unto

My
Deepest

Empty
Space

Evaporates

Every
Trace

Of

My
World's
Face.

In

Perfect
Empty

I
Remain.

The
Total
Loss,

Perfect
Gain.

All
Things,

Being
Relative,

There
Being

No
Size,
No
Duration,
No
Distance,
No
Prize,

Except

In
Arbitrary
Name,

Then

No
Thing
Is

'Real.'

Though

In

Mind's
Strong
Dream,

Any

Thing

May
So
Seem.

Perfection
Dawns.

A
Universe,

Dew
Drops

An
Eon,

Sparkle

A
Race,

On
The
Lawns

A
Wondrous
Scattering

Of
Space.

Of
Local
Place.

Each

Let
Us
Crawl,

With-
Draw,

Into

This
Heart,
Here,

Within

This
Atom
Spin,

Where-
In,

At
Point
Pure,

It's
Motions
Cease.

Here
Is
The

Silent
Pool
Of
Peace.

Here
Are
My

Pencil
And
Eraser,

The
Two
Forces

Elemental
And
Divine,

Cosmos
Creating :

Imagine
And
Ignore.

Start
New
And
Forget.

Growing
And
Death.

Create
And
Let
Go.

These   All

Movements   'Things'
Of
Breath,   That
                   I
These   Know.
Two,

Do
I,

And
So
Do

"The
Details
Escape
Me,"

He
Said.

"They
Are

All
Here,"

"But
Not

In
My
Head."

We
See
These
Things

Myriad,
Without
End,

And

We
Can't
Comprehend,

We
Who
Slumber.

But
To
You,

O
Perfect
True,

It
Is

Nothing,

To

Be
Without
Number.

Even
As
These

Waves

Rise
And
Fall,

Unmoving

Is

The
All.

Break
A
Hole

In
The
World.

Let
The
Time

Leak
Away.

Let
The
Infinite

In.

Let
World

Float
As
Fluff

On

The
Limitless

Wind.

O
Mind,

At
Rest,

Or

Some-
What
Still,

But
Going

To
And
Fro,

Where
E're
You
Will,

I
Find
You

To
Be

The
Best
Friend

At
Your
Borders,

Where

You
End.

The
Skin
Opens

Like
A
Dawn.

Like
A
Light,
Bright,

Turning
On.

I
Occupy

All
Sky,

Though

But
A

Momentary

Drop
Of
Dew,

A-
Shine

Upon
The
Lawn

Of

The
True.

The
World
You
See

Surrounding
Thee

Is

Part
Of
Thee,

Produced
Of
Thee.

It
Is
Thy
Shell,

Wherein
You
Dwell,

Thine
Own
Home,

Thine
Own
Heaven

Or
Hell,

The
Vicinity

Made
By
Thy

Mind's
Hand,

Thine
Own
Ability,

Thine
Own

Divine
Infinity,

O
Thou,
Most
Wondrous

Celestial,

Man.

In
Great
Flood,

In
Great
Shake,

In
Great
Whirling,

In
Great
Fire,

In
Pandemic
Panic,

Man
May
Strip

To
One
Desire.

To
Call
Upon

One
Perfect.

Kind.

Higher.

The
Empty
Arrives

Among
The
Busy.

The
True
Appears

Among
Apparitions.

Willingness
To
Cease

The
False

Grows
Clear.

Things
Solid

Grow
Sheer.

And
Perfect
Love

Is
Here.

One
Stream.

Many
Rocks.

One
Law

Of
The

Water
Fall.

Only
In

Perfection,

Can

What
Is

Be.

Some
Fall
Sudden

From
The
Tree,

Full
Ripe
And
Ready,

To
The
Core.

Some
Stay,

Ripen
Slow,

Day
By
Day,

A
Little
More,

Kissing
Sun

Until

All
Done.

For
Sure.

Please
O
Mind,

Do
Not
Be
Dull

To
The
Beauties

Of

A
Leaf.
A
Twig.

A
Pebble.
Or

A
Passing
Cloud.

The
Passing
Of
A
Day.

An
Eye.
A
Hand.

A
Heart.

The
All,

That

Flows
As
One.

O
Please,

Be
Alive

To
These.

You
May
See
It

In
The
Eyes.

But,

Maybe
Not,

For
It
Is

In

Divine
Disguise.

The
Normal
Man,

Made

To
Standard
Plan,

Though

He
Or
She

May

Know
It
Not,

At
Heart
Is

At
One.

Is
The
One,

All
Wise.

The
Wise
Say,

That

The
Man

Can

Contain,
Explain,

The
All,

And
This
Tell,

And
Yet

Remain

In
Mortal
Shell.

The
Infinite,

Including

Of
Course,

Zero
And
One,

Decides
To
Have
Some
Fun,

Puts
On
Costumes,

Stages
A
Play.

Here
It
Is.

It
Is
Called

'Today.'

Now

Are

All
Beginnings

One

With
Their
Endings.

Now
All
Payments

Received,

For
All

The
Lendings.

I
Am
Not

The
Broken
Bits

Of

Some
Explosion.

Nor

The
Empty
Space.

Nor
Some

Randomly
Gyrating
Motion.

And
I
Am

Neither

Wave,

Nor
Ocean.

O
Mind,

You
Would
Break

The
Continuum,
Perfect,

Into
Parcels,

Take
The
Data

To
Be

The
Real,

And

The
Map

To
Be

The
Terrain.

You   So,
Would

                       Say
Ignore   Plain,
The
True   How
                       Does
To   That
Maintain   Feel?

Thy   Is
Small   There
Domain.   Pain?

I
Look
Within,

The
Sage's
Eye,

And
All

Falls
Into
Place,

Free
Of

All

Time
And
Space.

Now
I
Am

The
Human
Race.

I
Am

First   All
Burst   Things
Of
Star.   Are.

I
Am

The
Only
One,

Who,

Ever,

Hey!

Can
You

Just
Stop

And

Do

Nothing ?

How
Hard
Could
That
Be?

Meeting

In

Gaze
Of
Sage,

Sudden
Light.

Persons
Vanish

With
The
Sight,

As

Shadows
Do

The
Mind
Ripens.

Reason

Grows
More
Neat,

As
Its
Season

Nears
Complete,

Just
Before

It
Grows
Soft,

Golden,

Juicy,
Sweet.

Unlimited,
Is,

In
Truth,

The
Man.

Though
He
May
Love

To
Plot
And
Plan,

And
Occupy

A
Certain
Place,

His
Home
Is
Ever

The
Perfect

Infinite
Space.

A
Child's
Hand

Wields,
Whirls,

An
Ember-
Ended
Stick

Upon
The
Dark.

A
Fiery
Spark

Circles,

Makes
A
Mark,

And,

So
Is
Whirled,

A
World.

So

A
Universe

Appears
To
Be,

Made
By

My
Hand,

Innocently.

There
Is
But

One

Atom
True,

Reflected,
Replicated,

Like
A
Full
Moon

On

A
Field
Of
Dew.

And
This
Is
True

Of

This
Orb
Of
Adam,

Too.

Grace

Comes
Dropping

Like
The
Dew.

Living
Droplets

Of

The
True.

O
Let
Us

Say
A
Blessing

On
This
Moment.

And
On
This.

And
This.

And

Let
Us

Open
And
Receive

This

Cosmic
Kiss.

Immerse,

O
Man,   For

Thy
Universe,   Nothing
                                           Is
In   Amiss.
This,

Perfection's
Kiss.

And,

Suffer
Not.

In
This
Infinity,

Perfect,
Complete,

Desires
All

Have
Met
Ends,
Sweet.

All
Circles
Closed.

All
Strangers,
Friends.

All
Deaths
Come

To
All
Those
Born.

All
Garments
Already
Worn.

The
Possibilities
Are

Already
Seen

In
Each
Recurring
Drama
Scene.

And
So,

O
Mortal
Man,

Why

Wish
And
Mourn?

Thou
Art

Ever

The
Pristine.

Releasing
Limits,

Turning
Walls
Enclosing
Spaces
Small,

To
Wings

That
Soar
Infinity,

Releasing
All

Identity,

The
Being

Disappears

Into
Its
Seeing,

With

Nothing
Left
To
See,

So

Finds
The
Bliss

At
Border
Lands,

Where
Being

Used
To
Be.

O,

Smile!

The
Treasure
Keeper

Has
Placed
All

In
The
Safe,

With

The
Combination

Marked

On
The
Dial.

O
Hear

The

Xylophone
Of
Heaven

Ring.

Creating

Every
Thing.

Hear
The

Angel

Harp
String

Play,

Reverberating,

As

This
Day.

All
Of
Outer
Space,

Deepest
Sleep
Of
Night,

Falls
Into
The
Man,

Though

Day

Be
Bright.

Now
The
Still

Fills

All
In
Sight.

A
Fountain

Flows.

A
Mountain

Glows.

A
Mind
Wave

Seeks.
Peaks.

Knows.

Silence
Comes

Upon
The
Man.

Distinctions,

He
Had
Made,

Fade,

De-
Construe,

Un-
True.

Traction
Slips

Into
The
Sea.

The
Tranquility.

The
Two,

The

Me
And
You,

Dissolve
Into
The
One.

The
True.

Mind
Would
Divide

Man
And
God,

And
Make
Infinity

Seem

Alien
And
Odd,

And
Make
Man

Seem
To
Be

Only

Son
And
Daughter

Of
The
Sod.

Infinity,

O,

You
Tricky
Knot,

Some
How,

You
Are
So

Obvious,

That

Among
Man,

Here,

You
Are

Forgot.

Into
The

Stationary

Center
Of
All,

Mind
Doth
Fall.

In
This

Silence,

No
Desires
Call.

Infinity
Has

Fulfilled
Them
All.

Here
Is
A
Net,

That,

Cast
Into
The
Sea,

On
Catching
The
Fish,

Sets

Them

Free.

O
Man,

Busy
One,

Our
Most
Important
Task

Is

To
Pause,

And
Ask.

And
Then,
But

To
Bask.

Awash

In
Infinitude's

Peace
Perfect,

The
Scene
Blows
Open,

The
All-
Inclusive,

Now
Learned,

Making
Irrelevant

The
Mere

Discerned.

A
Story

Carved
In
Stone

Remains,

Though,

This
Glyph
And
Picture

After
Time,

None
Explains.

As,
Even
At
Last,

The
Very
Mountain
Chains

Have

Drifted
Off,

Just

A
Smoky
Haze,

In
This

Long

And

Never-
Ending

Passing
Away

Of
Ways.

O
Man,

At
Death's
Moment,

When

Limitations
Are
Deserting
You

As
You
Sink

Into

The
Sky
Of
You,

Breaking
Open
Bound-
Less,

And
Your
Place
Of
Rest

No
Longer
Has
Sheets,

Or
A
Sleeper,

Here

You
May
Arrive

Even
Right
Now,

Ready
To
Go,

Deeper.

Now

Mind's
Temple

I
Raise,

A
Stonehenge,

Around
Me,

Under
Open
Sky.

And
My

Great
Stones
Fly

Aloft
Upon

Wind
Soft.

And
In
This

Galaxy
Round,

Where-
In,

Inside

Now
I
Ride,

I
May
Stay,
Reside,

While

Here
Am
I

High

On
This

Promontory,

Above
The
Momentary

Tide.

Into

Mind's
Campfire

I
Toss

Thought's
Stick.

Long
And
Dark,

Or

Short
And
Thick,

Each
Taking

The
Fire

Brighter,

Quick.

Here
Is

A
Universe

In
A

Size-
Less
Point,

Held
Now,
There,

In

A
Decision

To
Let
It
Be,

By

The
True
Me,

The
All
Aware.

Wait.

Here
Is
A
Door.

We
Can
Exit
Here,

Or,

If
You
Prefer,

Now
Forbear,

And
More

Of

This

End-
Less-
Ness

Explore.

Infinite

Are

The
Amazing
Ways

Of

Remembering

To
Be

The

Changeless
One.

An
Inch,

Or,

A
Parsec,

A
Parsec
Of
Parsecs.

The
Atom's

Mid-
Most

Atom-
Point
Inside.

The
Impossibly
Small.

The
Impossibly
Wide.

All

In
My
Mind

Now
Reside

And
Play.

And
All

But
Say,

'Who
  Am
   I?'

Every
Circle

Is

The
Same,

Regardless
Of

Its

Size
Or
Name.

Atom's
Smallest
Inner
Spot,

Or
Galaxy
Of
Stately
Spin,

Or,

This
Ululating
Thought

Of
Mine,

Now
Spinning,

Seemingly

'Within.'

The
Infinite
Bliss

Is
Bundled

Into
Parcels,

In
Eye
Of
Man,

Now
So
Rapt.

The
Brilliance,

The
Perfection
Of
God,

Shining
In
Man,

Though
He
Goes

In
Mortal
Clothes,

Ever
Leads
Him

Better

Than

He
Knows.

The
Storm
Of
Desire

Sweeps
In,

Flooding
The
Calm

With
Windy
Waves,

Making
All

Thought

Its
Slaves.

Blindness
Darkens
Light.

Mind,
Blind,

Pronounces

Day
To
Be

Night.

An
Island
Of
Ignoring

Defends
Its
Own

Shortness
Of
Sight.

Yes,

That

The
Man

No
Sky

Who

Hugs
The
Ground

Can
Be
Found.

May
Say

Here
Is

The
Man,

A
Mere

Cloud
Formation,

Drifting
Sky
Pattern

Passing
By,

The
Momentary
I,

Coalesced

In
The
Clear

Infinite

Wide
And
High.

The
Man

Struggles
Through

The
Cocoon

Of

His
Own
Spinning,

Leaving
It
Behind,

Finally
Winning,

And
No
Longer

What
He
Or
She
Was.

Now
To
Fly,

As

A
Daze
Of
Ambrosias

Flits
By.

And
Then,

The
Empty
Sky,

Wings
Left
Also
Behind.

Beautiful,

But
Dry.

I
Saw
You
Smile,

O
Sky.

It
Lingered

For
A
While,

There
In
The

Brilliant
Blue,

To
Convince
Us

It
Was
True.

Some
Of
Us
Saw,

And

Smiled
With
You.

Into

Spine's
Stick,

Zero
Thick,

Divine
Light's

Candle
Wick,

I
With-
Draw,

To
Be

First
Axis
Line,

Infinite
Fine,

Of

First
Atom

To
Define.

And
Here,

In
This

Peace,

I
Cease

To
Be
First
Form,

I
Cease
To
Adhere.

Now
As

The
Infinite
Perfect

Clear.

The
Mind,
Centered,

Is
Not
Sized.

Any
Size

Could
Be
Surmised.

Here,
In
This
Spot,

Infinity
And
Zero

Join
At
One.

O
Mind,

You
May

Rest
Here.

Now

That
Your

Wonder
Wander

Relativity
Journey

Finally

Is
Done.

Anchor
Cannot
Grip

The
Bottom-
Less.

Wave
Can
Not

Tip
Ship

That
Is

Come
To
Be

Already
Sunk.

Already

Sea.

Now
Doth

All
Activity

Pause,

Re-
Connect
To,

Become,

Its
Cause.

Climb,

O
Jack,

Thy
Bean
Stalk,

Growing
High.

Bring
Back
Now

Thy
Giant

From
The
Sky.

O
Fear
Not,

For

He
Is
Thee.

Thine
Own

I.

No
Need

To

Fear
Or
Fly.

Steady
Star,

Above,
Far,

Please,
Guide.

For,

My
Ocean
Here

Is
Wide.

Proud
And
Loud,

Day

Widens

Out
Of
Dawn.

But,
O

I
Feel

The
Deep

Night
Silence,

Never
Gone.

Thought
With
Wing

With

Wide
As
Sky

My

'I'.

Now
Doth
Fly,

Soaring
Away

Blue
And
White

A
Planet
Ball

Graceful

Turns

Within
The
All.

O

First
Fluctuation

In

The
Still,

Now,

A
Universe,

You
Fill.

As
I
Focus

In
Small
Task,

Let
Me

In
Thee

Bask,

O
Perfect
True.

This
Is

All

I
Ask.

The
Stationary

Holds

The
Moving.

The
Silence
In
The
Word,

The
True

Is
Proving.

The
Deep
Sky

Comes

Dropping
In,

Peace
Deep
Raining,

Through
The
Man,

Through
Every
Thing.

No
Distinctions

Remaining.

A
Man
Sits

Only
Me.

Beneath,

Within,

My
Silence.

At
Last
Listening,

Accepting,
Absorbing,
Being,

O

Whirling
World,

That

Rotate
And
Revolve,

And
Evolve,

In
The
Problems

That
Arise,

It
Is

Who
You
Are,

That
You
Are

To
Solve.

The
Stationary

Guides

The
Moving.

Only

This,

The
Way
True,

Proving.

It
Is
Morning.

The
Day

Now

Breaks
Open

Bright.

Breaks
Apart

Into
Pieces,

Into
Infinity,

The
Silence

Of

The
Night.

Before

First
Creature
Came,

All

Had
One
Name.

O
See,

Even
In

This
Moment
Now,

It
Is

Yet

The
Same.

The

Man
Skin

Goes
Thin.

Drifts

On

Infinite
Wind,

A

Cipher
Of
Mist

In
Sky,

Widening
Away

Upon

The
High.

Do
I

Occupy

This

Tiny
Spot,

A
Merest
Dot

Within
This

Vast
And
Deep

Infinity?

O,
Let
Me
See.

Which
Of
These,

In

All
Of
These

Nests
Of
Infinities,

Contains

This
Me?

Man
On
Planet

Rides
Time's
Tides,

Finds

The
Narrows

And

The
Wides.

Man's
Eyes
May
Go

The
Breadth
Of
Skies

And

Into
Atom's
Fine
Insides.

But,
O,

Let
The
Man

Self

See,

Besides.

O
Mind,

Let
Not

Thine
Old

Ignoring,
Boring,

Get
In

Thy
Way.

Put
Shadow
Away.

Be

The
Whole
Day.

Mind
Stays,
Plays,

Splays
Its
Displays,

Within

These
Local

Nights
And
Days,

While,

Ever,
Soft,

Soul
Lifts
Aloft

In
Subtle
Air

Where

Perfection

Stays.

O

Let
No

Imagined
Size

Mesmerize

Thine
Eyes.

For,

Size
Is

All
Same,

A
Play

In
A

Relativity
Game.

Man
Mind

Picks
One,

Moves
In,

And

Gives
It
A
Name.

I

Carve
A
Cave

In
This

So
Solid

Time
And
Space.

In
This

Midst

Of

Daily
Living's

Fevered
Race,

I
Have
My

Perfect
Quiet
Place.

Now.

The
Still
Spot.

Size-
Less,
Place-
Less,

At
Center,

I

Enter.

The

Still
Spot

Size-
Less,
Place-
Less,

Time-
Less,

Ever
I

Occupy.

From

The
One

Tranquil
Heart,

All
Things

Start,

Though

The
Man

May
See

Only
Part.

I,

Infinite
Sky,

Descend,

Touch,

Rest
In,
Upon,

This

Form
Of
Man,

This

Bit
Of
Wave,

Bit
Of
Dust,

Brief

Glittering
Of
Light,

An
Instant

In

My
Perfect
Night,

Here

In

My
Perfect

Bright.

A
Wave

Comes
In,

Washes,

Goes
Out.

A
Day,

An
Idea,

A
World,

A
Star.

Such

A
Wave
As
This,

Is
This

O
Man,

What
You
Are?

'Who
Am
I ?'

One
Asks.

There
Was
Here

A
Man,

Answering,

Problem
Solved,

Just

As
He

Dissolved.

Release

Unto
Peace.

Let
The
Murmuring

Cease.

Let
Fall
Thrall.

Terminate

Lease.

Perfect
Balance

To
Make,

May
Require

A
Give,

Where
There

Was
Take.

O
Mind,

Gather
Thy
Threads.

Attend
Thy
Loom.

Weave

Thy
Tapestry.

Adorn

Thy
Room.

Unto
The
Self

The
Man
Creeps,

Bee
In
Flower,

Heaven's
Nectar
Scent

In
Full
Power.

Man

In
Ecstasy

This
Hour.

The
Cup
Of
Oneness

Comes
To
Lip,

Heavenly
Aroma
Here.

O
Mind,

Ambrosia

Is
Yours
Today.

Take

The
Sip.

A
Window

Opens

In
Time's
Room.

Day
Light

Floods
Away

Old
Gloom.

Here
Is
Freedom,

Where
Was

Doom.

Mind
Object

Bubbles

Pop.

Concept
Foaming

Comes
To

Stop.

No
Man
More

Mortal
Is,

As

All
Contained
Ideas

Drop.

Come
To
Harbor.

Come
To
Shore.

Stormy
Tossing
Sea,

Cross
No
More.

Here
At
Last

Is
Stillness

Pure.

Here

Arrive
Alive,

O
Ye
Of

Course

Guided
Sure.

The
Man

Breaks
Up

And

Dissolves,

Resolves
Into

Perfect

Light
And
Sound.

And,

Falling
Still

More
Profound,

Is

The
Quiet

All
Around.

The

Point
Of
View

Lifts
Away.

Flies
Out
Far.

The
Man
Is

But

A
Blip.

Earth,
A
Grain
Of
Sand.

And
The
Sun,

A
Tiny
Point.

A
Very

Distant
Star.

Who
Says

This

Is
Not

How
Things
Are?

Within
The
Middle

Of

The
Divide,

I
Ride,

Stillness
Poised

Within
The
Tide,

Here,

At
The
Quiet

Wherein

All
Things

Reside.

It
Is
Wise

To
Realize

That

Each
Degree
Of
Size

Lies

Only
In

The
Beholder's
Eyes.

A
Physical
Body
Self,

A
Society
Self,

A
Man-
Kind
Self,

The
Nature
Elf,
Self,

The
Law
Of
Form
Self,

The
Light
Of
Seeing
Self,

Inhabit

Any
And

All

Of
These,

As
You
Please,

O
Mind,

Or,

Leave
All

On
The
Shelf.

This
Entire
Man,

This
Whole
Race,

This

Entire
Life

In
This
Place,

Is

But
A
Wrinkle

On
The
Brow,

Now,

Of
My

Perfect
Face,

A
Wriggle

Of

A
Light
Wave

In

My
Perfect
Space.

Perfection
Ever
Is,

The
Infinite,
Serene,

Not
To
Be

Forgotten

When

But
Partial
Things

Are
Seen.

You   The
Are   Treasures

My   Thou
Dearest   Art
Pearl,   Worth.

O
Little
Earth,

For
I
Know

I,

Perfect
Sky,

Clear,

Here
Congeal

To
Be

Man
On
Sphere,

To
Enjoy,

To
Conceal

The
Infinite
Display

Within
This
Day,

Just
To

Feel

The
Breeze,

And
To
See

The
Infinite

Dancing
Leaves

At
Play.

Let

Mind
Roam,

But

Bring
It
Home,

Back
To

The
Total
True.

Let
It

Cease
To
Do,

And
Only
Be,

Silently,

Beyond
The
Busy

Of

Infinity.

This
Palm
Tree

Rises
On
A
Line,

A
Spine

Like
Mine,

Centered
In

A
Straightness
Fine,

And,

At
Top

Bursts,

Splays,
Plays,

Displays
Its
Rays,

Arrays
Its
Self

In
Praise.

So
Like
Me,

It
Prays.

In

The
Stillness,

One
Vibration

Moves,

And
So,

The
Silence

Proves.

Gratitude.

I
Bask.

A
Warming
Sun

In
Silence.

What
More

Could
One
Ask?

Now

Objects
All

Fall

Into
A
Glittering

Of
Sparkles,

That

Glitter
All
Away.

Time
And
Space

Have

Had
Their
Day.

O
Mind

You
Will
Find

The
Main
Job

Is
This:

To
Be

In
Bliss.

To
Feel

Perfection's
Kiss.

The
Space
Shape

Around

The
Thing,
Or
The
Man,

Holds,
Feels,
Sees,

Every
Nook

And
Cranny,

Every

Wrinkle
In
The
Skin,

All
The

Hollow
Spaces,

Every　　　　　Has
Bend,　　　　　No
　　　　　　　　Back,
Around,
Within.　　　　No
　　　　　　　　End.

And
Note,

The
Space
Shape

The

'Things
To
Do'

List,

Not
Pauses,

But
Poises

In
Grace,

Moving
Yet
Still,

As

All
Things
Are,

Even
Now,

Perfectly

In
Place.

No
Going.

No
Waiting.

No
Changing.

No
Needing

Is.

Now
And
Here

The
Perfect

Is.

When

Infinity
Has
Come

To
Fill

Your
Coffer,

What
Else

Could
Another

Offer?

The
Grace
Falls,

Ever

Sweet.

Blessings
Un-
Bidden

Land
At
Feet.

Now,

Gone
Golden,

The
Simple
Path

Is

Palatial
Street.

O
Angel,

Dear,

I
Feel
You

Near.

I
Feel

Your

All
Raw
Awe,

Now

So
Clear.

Beauty
Hovers

Every
Where,

In
The
Earth,

In
The
Air,

In
The
Sorrow,

In
The
Prayer.

O
Mind,

Be
Now
But

First
Star.

Broad-
Cast
Now

All
Things
That
Are.

Be
Still
Point,

The

Ultimate
Small.

Be

Farthest
Farthest
Far.

Be

Tallest   None
Tall.   Of
                 These
See
That   At
You   All.
Be

The
Silent
True,

So,

The
Emptiness

Falls
Through,

Mid-
Man,

Thought,
Feeling,
Existence,

Gone.

Sparks
Scintillate,
Fall,
Evaporate,

Atmosphere
Gone
Space.

No
Man
Here,

But
Only

The
Only

Ever
True,

Source
Spring

Of

This
Falling

Fall
Of
Grace.

Two
Seconds

Pass.

A
Minute
And
A
Half.

An
Hour
And
Ten
Minutes.

O.

An
Entire
After-
Noon.

And
Soon,

Three
Days,

Five
Weeks,

Ten
Years,

A
Life-
Time-
Long.

Gone.

Like
A
Song
Played.

And

We
Had
Thought

It
Stayed.

I,

Silent
Sky,

End-
Less
Space,

All,

Now

Silently

Embrace.

One

Is
Disguised

As
Being

Two.

What,

O

Mind,

Does
This
Do

To
You?

O,

You
Who
Compose

The
Budding
Rose,

I
Do
Love

So
Well.

With
You

Would
I

For
Ever

Dwell,

As

One

Cascading,

Perfect

Petal
Shell.

This
Moment

Has
Been
Waiting

Here,

Lodged
In

The
Winding
Mines
Of
Time,

A
Diamond
Clear

Of

Surpassing
Worth.

Perfection

In

The
Darkened
Earth.

Now,

Upon
The

Labyrinth

Infinite
Perfect,

That
Doth
So

Amaze,

I
Gaze.

World's
Illusions

Toil
And
Spin,

While

The
Perfect
True

Ever
Shines,

All,
Within.

Upon
Infinity's

Zero
Balance

Razor
Edge,

Is

Each
Thing

That
Mind
May

See
Or
Sense.

The
Subtle-
Most,

The
Most
Dense.

At
This

Zero

Do   As
All
Things
                They
End,   Commence.

As
They
Exist,

And

The
Ultimate
End
Time,

Waited
For

By
Some,

Is,

Of
Course,

Already
Come.

The
End
Times.

The
Origin
Times,

These
Want
Not,

Wait
Not,

For

A
Man's

Small
Seeing,

To
Have

Their
Being.

Many

Lives
And
Languages

Of
Old

Soft
Are
Laid

Within
This

Earthly
Garment
Fold.

Some
Few
Are
Known

By
Us
Today,

But
Most

By
Far

Are
Lost
Among

The
Un-
Told.

A
Stone,

A
Bone,

All
That
Is
Found

Of
A
Tale,

A
Life,

That
Was
Once

Long
And
Profound.

The
Sun,

Now
Inebriate

On

Its
Own
Core,

Bursts
With
Shining

Ever
More.

Stands
In
The
Silence

Of

Its
Own
Roar.

Eternity's
Road,

That
Was

Endless
Ahead,

Lies
Now

Here,

In
My

Palm,

Instead.

In

The
Giving,

The
Man

Joins

The
Source

Of
Living.

Tumblers
Click,

Fall
Into
Place,

And

A
Lock
Lands,

The
Combination
Learned,

Free

To
Be
Freely
Turned.

Now

Swing
Open
The
Door

To
The

For-
Ever
More.

Be
We
But

A

Proto-
Plasm
On
A
Rock,

Rounding
Its
Rings
Around
A
Star?

O

Let
Us
Not
Be
Fooled

By

What
We
Sense

Among
Things

The
Most
Dense,

The
Least
Immense,

That
Are.

Battle
Lines
Are
Formed.

'Me
And
Thee,'

Iron
Filing
Souls

'Yea
And
Nay.'

Line
Up
In
Array

Here
It
Is,

Around

Like
This,

Magnet
Poles
Of

Yet
Another
Day.

O

Abdicate
Not

Thine
Own

Throne.

It
Is

Thine
Alone.

Be
Pleased

To
Sit.

Do
Not

It

To
Another

Loan.

O
Man

What
Do
You
Hear
There

In
Your
Head?

What
Would
You

Choose

To
Be
There

Instead?

The
Perfect
True

Or
More
Of

What
You've
Been
Fed?

Will
You
Explore?

Or,

Will
You
Be
Led?

Now

The
Edges

Of
The
Moment

Stretch
Away

Unto
The

End-
Less-
Ness.

No
Man
Is.

But
Only

The
First
Stuff

Is
Here,

And
A
Temporary
Hovering

In

The
Clear.

The
Cycle
Turns.

Moon
Shines.

Sun
Burns.

Night
And
Day

Chase
Each
Other

Away.

Ups
And
Downs

Play.

In

All
Of
These,

Serene
And
Still

I

Stay.

Prolong

The
Agony.

Or,

Drop
Now

Into
Bliss.

O,

The
Choice

Is
This.

Let
Us
Go

Out

To
The
Desert,

Where

Every
Stone
Is
Pristine,

Where

Every
Star
Is
Seen.

Where
Mind
Of
Man

May
Be
Silent
And
Clean.

The
Serene.

O,
Look!

It
Is

Raining
Jewels.

Divide,

O
My
Dear

Mind
Divine.

O
Make

First
Mark.

Make
First

Spark
In
Dark.

Separate

Into
A
Two.

And
Then,

Please,

Proliferate.

O   To

Let   Be
Us   And
Have   Do.

An
Infinity

Of
Things

O
Mind,

So
Accustomed
Are
You,

To

Seeking
A
Domicile.

Any
Small
Hut

will
Do.

Or

A
Palace,

Preening,
Teeming,

Perchance.

Any
Set
Of

Walls
And
Floor,

Roof
And
Door,

For
You

To
Hold

Onto.

Every

Man
Bud

Blossoms,

Flowers
Forth

In

Its
Own
Way.

All
Are
OK.

All
Are

The
Divine
One

At
Play,

And
For
Ever

Do

So
Stay.

This
Myriad,

Nothing

Here,

Amiss.

In
The
One

Quiescence,

Perturbs

But
As

A
Bliss.

As
The

Stillness

Washes
Through,

The
Man
World

Sparkles.

New.

Uniqueness
Perfect

Penetrates

This
Infinity.

Perfect
Diversity,

An
Actuality

Of
Singularity.

There
Is
No
Slow.

There
Is
No
Fast.

There
Is

No
Future

Nor
A
Past.

There
Is
No
Place.

There
Is
No
Size.

All
These
Exist

Only
In

A
Personal

Delusion's

Eyes.

Habits

Are
Placed
There

With
Care.

Lists
Of
What
To
Do.

Verbal
Prompts

Of
Where

Next
To
Go.

These
Ensure
That

The
Man
Is

Tracking
World,

Through   There
The   To
Day,   Stay.

Lest
The
Mind
May

Slip
Utterly
Away

Unto

Peace
Perfect,

I
Am

The

Peace
Perfect,

That
Contains

All
These
Oscillating
Schemes,

That,

So
It
Seems,

Emerge
As

These

So
Solid
Dreams.

Chords
Of
Conscious-
Ness

Play
Their
Sound

Profound,

Variations
On
A
Theme

That
All

Seem
To
Say,

The
One-
Ness

Here
Is
Seen,

Yet
Again,

Another
Way.

Though

Infinity's
Dream

Would
Seem

To

Intervene,

Ever,

Remain
I,

The
Pristine.

Perfection
Rules,

By
Man

Holds
What
Is

Confused

By
Seeing
Life
Diffused,

In
Place,

Though
This
May

Through

Not
Be
Seen

Time
And
Space.

Among,
Between,

Ever,

The
Diverse

I,

Ever-
Moving

The
Quiescent,

My
Silence

Infinity
Of
Thing,

Sing.

ABOUT THE AUTHOR

 Who is this Author?

This question is best answered by looking into the author's finished pages, which stand ready for the reading.

But, in the interests of social convention, here is some biographical data to clothe this character.

The early years of the author were steeped in several cultures.

The author as a youngster spent long hours and years in the laconic hard scrabble labor of rural Appalachian mountain life, his father's roots.

The author's mother came from the prosperous flatter farmlands of rural Maryland, close-knit family people of an old Pennsylvania Dutch background, who sang sweet acapela harmonies, while praying and working together.

The author grew up in both influences, while living in the midst of the robust cultural mix of the Washington D.C. environs.

The author left high school blessed with a scholarship to an exceptionally fine university, where he spent his four years, wandering somewhat, among the peaks of Man's intellectual achievement.

The Writing Seminars were among the most memorable experiences of the time there, hours of sharing words among fellow poets, lounging around a large and darkly aged conference table.

In the cultural uproar of the 1968-69 senior year, studies were eclipsed, as the author's interests exploded into off-campus venues and activities, not in the political actions of the day, but in the spiritual, metaphysical and transcendental.

In this vibrant time, the City of Baltimore burgeoned with opportunities for close friendships, learning and practice with various yogis from India, gypsies, highly conscious artists and mystics of various kinds, along with a matured Theosophical Lodge and Rosicrucian Lodge, AMORC, all of this guided by the posters and amazingly well-stocked shelves of the New Age Bookstore, where meditators gathered, crowded together seated on the floor on Tuesday evenings. The author was a part of spiritual communes that started up and renovated spaces in which to work and live together.

This storm of Baltimore life came on, seemed to last forever, and then passed suddenly, with an abrupt departure to a place in Vermont's north woods.

Then stretched decades of living various places, supported by working with hands and small building business activity, with years of life's lessons in family living with children, years of a spiritual-martial practice, years spent close with a guru from India, and years of working with a spiritually oriented mind training course.

In recent years, the art of word-craft, practiced since childhood, came to the fore.

A body of privately written work slowly accumulated, waiting for the writer to feel ready for its release.

FROM THE PUBLISHER

Hello, Dear Reader!

We hope that you have enjoyed *Rise Eyes Wise*!

This is the third book in a series of three. Perhaps you have experienced the different flavors of the other two books, *Falling Into All* and *Prayer Sayer Song*.

We would like to request your help, once again. If you enjoy *Rise Eyes Wise*, will you please be so kind as to let your kindred spirits know? Will you post a review where you purchased your copy, or on Amazon?

Remember, if you have not already done so, you can download your free copy of the ebook called *Forever Free*.

Get it here:

www.WiseWordWind.com.

You can also sign up to receive fresh single pages weekly from Ben, in your inbox or on social media.

If you would like to connect with Ben, you can email him at Ben@WiseWordWind.com.

Thank you!

-The Team at Wise Word Wind Press